OUR STORY

First published in Great Britain in 2025 by John Murray (Publishers)

1

Copyright © Colin Butfield and Jonnie Hughes 2025

The right of Colin Butfield and Jonnie Hughes to be identified as the Author of the Work has been asserted by them in accordance with the Copyright, Designs and Patents Act 1988.

All rights reserved. No part of this publication may be reproduced, stored in a retrieval system, or transmitted, in any form or by any means without the prior written permission of the publisher, nor be otherwise circulated in any form of binding or cover other than that in which it is published and without a similar condition being imposed on the subsequent purchaser.

A CIP catalogue record for this title is available from the British Library

Hardback ISBN 978 1 399 83500 8

Typeset in NHM Wallop
Printed and bound in Italy by L.E.G.O. Spa

John Murray policy is to use papers that are natural, renewable and recyclable products and made from wood grown in sustainable forests. The logging and manufacturing processes are expected to conform to the environmental regulations of the country of origin.

Carmelite House
50 Victoria Embankment
London EC4Y 0DZ

www.johnmurraypress.co.uk

John Murray Press,
part of Hodder & Stoughton Limited
An Hachette UK company

The authorised representative in the EEA is Hachette Ireland, 8 Castlecourt Centre, Dublin 15, D15 XTP3, Ireland (email: info@hbgi.ie)

Acknowledgements

This book is based on the script for the immersive experience 'Our Story' with David Attenborough written by Colin Butfield and Jonnie Hughes.

The immersive was produced by Open Planet Studios and co-funded by

 and

Designed by
Luke Halls Studios

Executive Produced and Directed by
Jonnie Hughes
Colin Butfield

Original Music Composed by
Nick Powell

Sound Design
Gareth Fry

Researcher
Kate Streather

For Luke Halls Studios

Creative Director
Luke Halls

Producer
Charlotte Wilde

Artists
Luca Brenna
Graham Bucknell
Cem Duz
James Harford
Karol Marcinkowski
Berk Polat

For Open Planet Studios

Director of Operations
Andrew McKerlie

Production Manager
Samantha Cook

Head of Technical Operations
Daniel Beare

Technical Manager
Mick Heath

Directed and Produced by
Victoria Bromley

Assistant Producer
Annie Moir

Archive Producers
Maggie Oakley
Lawrence Breen

Editor
Steve Phillips

Development Producer
Elliot Jenkins

Head of Production
Helen Healy

Junior Production Manager
Daniel Byers

Technical Lead
Mark Phippen

Production Accountant
Rubie Kent

Scientific Advisors
Stephen Axford and Catherine Marciniak/Planet Fungi, Dr Patrick Hickey/Hypha Research Limited, Dr Grace Russell, Edda Elísabet Magnúsdóttir, Society for the Protection of Underground Networks (SPUN), Natural History Museum

Archive Acknowledgements
Aerialcollection for GoodPlanet Foundation, Alfredo Barroso, BBC Motion Gallery/Getty Images, BFI National Archive, Bob Campbell Papers/George A. Smathers Libraries/University of Florida, Getty Images, Hans Hass Archive, Jane Goodall Institute, Kinolibrary, Kyle Roepke, Alexander Matthew/Dr Anne Innis Dagg Estate, Johnny Miller/Unequal Scenes, NASA, Nuno Sá, Open Planet Library, Overview, Pond5, Screenocean/Historic Films, Silverback Films, Steve Wall, WWF

Book Design
Dave Brown @ ApeInc.Co.Uk

Picture Credits

The following credit list refers to the images as they are located on each double-page spread from numbers 1 to 46. 47 refers to the final single page.

Front cover: © Shutterstock.com and Science Photo Library. **Endpapers:** © Luke Halls Studio. **Inside:** Alamy Stock Images: 23/ Iakov Filimonov; 28 top left/ Ivy Close Images, bottom left/ Florilegius, top right/ World History Archive, top far right/ Historic Illustrations, centre right/ Walker Art Library, bottom right/ North Wind Picture Archives, all remaining images/ Central Historic Books; 29 all, top left/ Central Historic Books, top centre/ Science History Images, bottom centre left, Piemags/rmn, bottom right, INTERFOTO; 34 left/ Tomas Griger; 36 left/ LightField Studios Inc., right/ Amazing Aerial; 37 left/ NicoElNino; 39/ NPS Photo; 40/ mauritius images GmbH; 43/ imageBROKER.com; 44/ Cosmo Condina. Getty Images: 13/ Jackyenjoyphotography; 14 far left/MARK GARLICK/SCIENCE PHOTO LIBRARY; left/Pablo Carlos Budassi/Stocktrek Images, centre left/ aryos, centre right/SCIEPRO/SCIENCE PHOTO LIBRARY; 19/ Ippei Naoi; 20/ PT STOCK; 21/ Anup Shah; 22/ Maika 777; 24 left/ Juan Maria Coy Vergara; centre /Twenty47studio; right /Darryl Leniuk; 25/ Abstract Aerial Art; 26 top left/ Beata Whitehead, centre left/ Francois Gohier/VW Pics/Universal Images Group, bottom left/ Manoj Shah, top centre/ Jacky Parker Photography, centre /Images say more about me than words, centre bottom/ Georgette Douwma, top right/ georgeclerk, centre right/ Nick Brundle Photography, bottom right/ TCYuen; 33 left/ Narumon Bowonkitwanchai; 35 left/ Stuart Fox; 38 top/ Andrew Merry, bottom/ Artur Debat; 41/ by wildestanimal; 42/ Paul Souders; 44/ SamBarnes; 45/ John Seaton Callahan; 46/ Olga Rolenko. Created by Luke Halls Studio: 1–10, 14 right, 15–18, 27, 30, 33, 47/ Our Story 25 Ltd, 11–12/ Oceans 25 Ltd, 31–32/NASA. Created by Daily Overview: source imagery © Maxar 33 right/ Bingham Canyon Mine, 34 right/ Bolivian Deforestation, 35 right/ Ankara Residential Development; source imagery © Nearmap 37 right/ Houston Abandoned Cars.

OUR STORY

The Remarkable Tale of an Extraordinary Species

Colin Butfield & Jonnie Hughes

It's

easy

to

question

our

significance.

What is our place in all of this?

What is our purpose?

What is our story?

What are each of us,

or indeed all of us together,

when considered

in the vastness

of space and time?

The fact is we *are* significant,
even in the universe,
because our home,
Earth, is significant.

And Earth, in turn,
is significant because of us.

There are billions of planets in the universe.

The vast majority are likely to be lifeless worlds.

Once upon a time, Earth was just another among them:

unstable, hostile,

but unlike all the other planets

of which we have knowledge,

Earth's story has other chapters.

And those chapters were written by life.

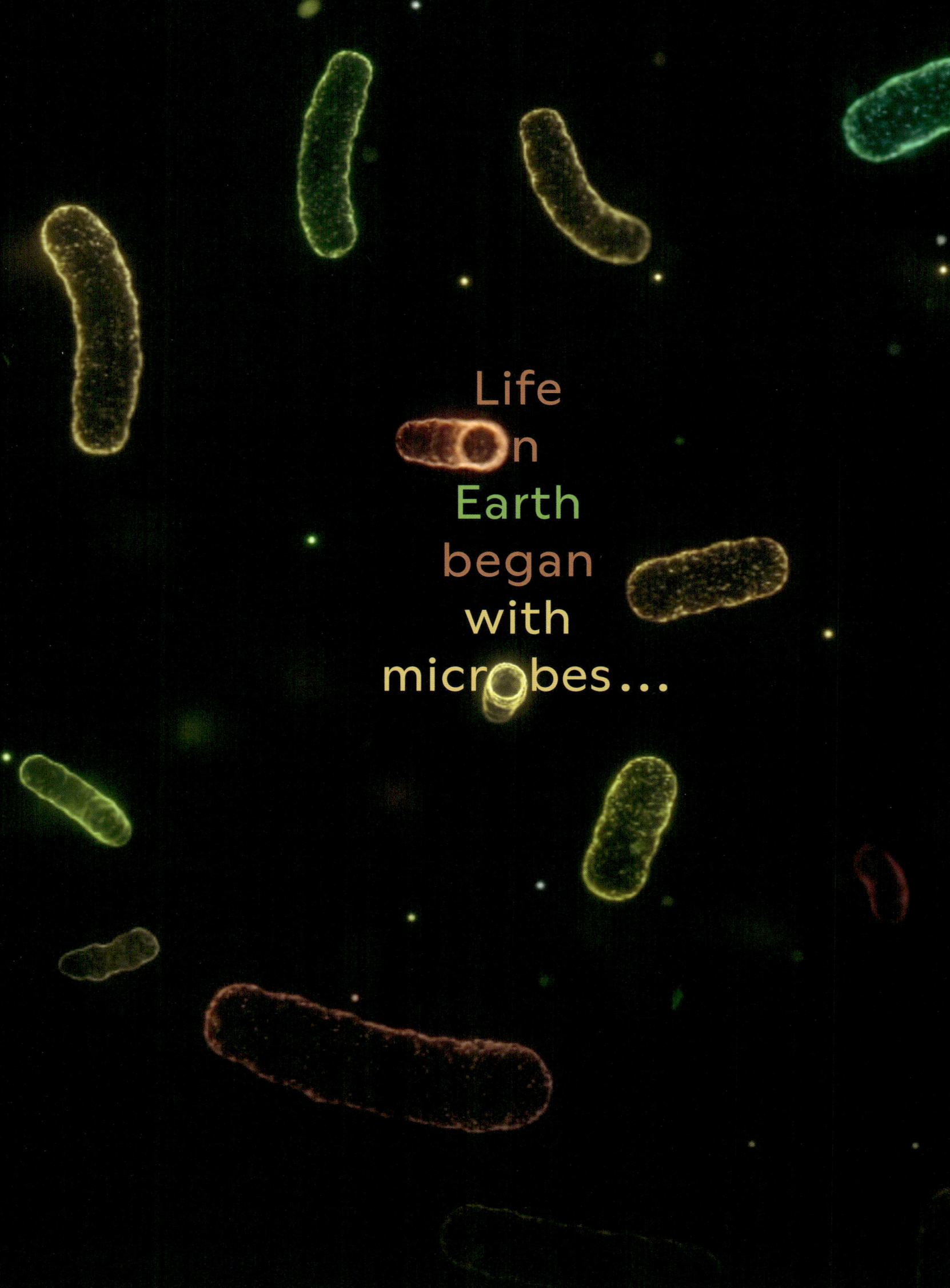

Life
on
Earth
began
with
microbes…

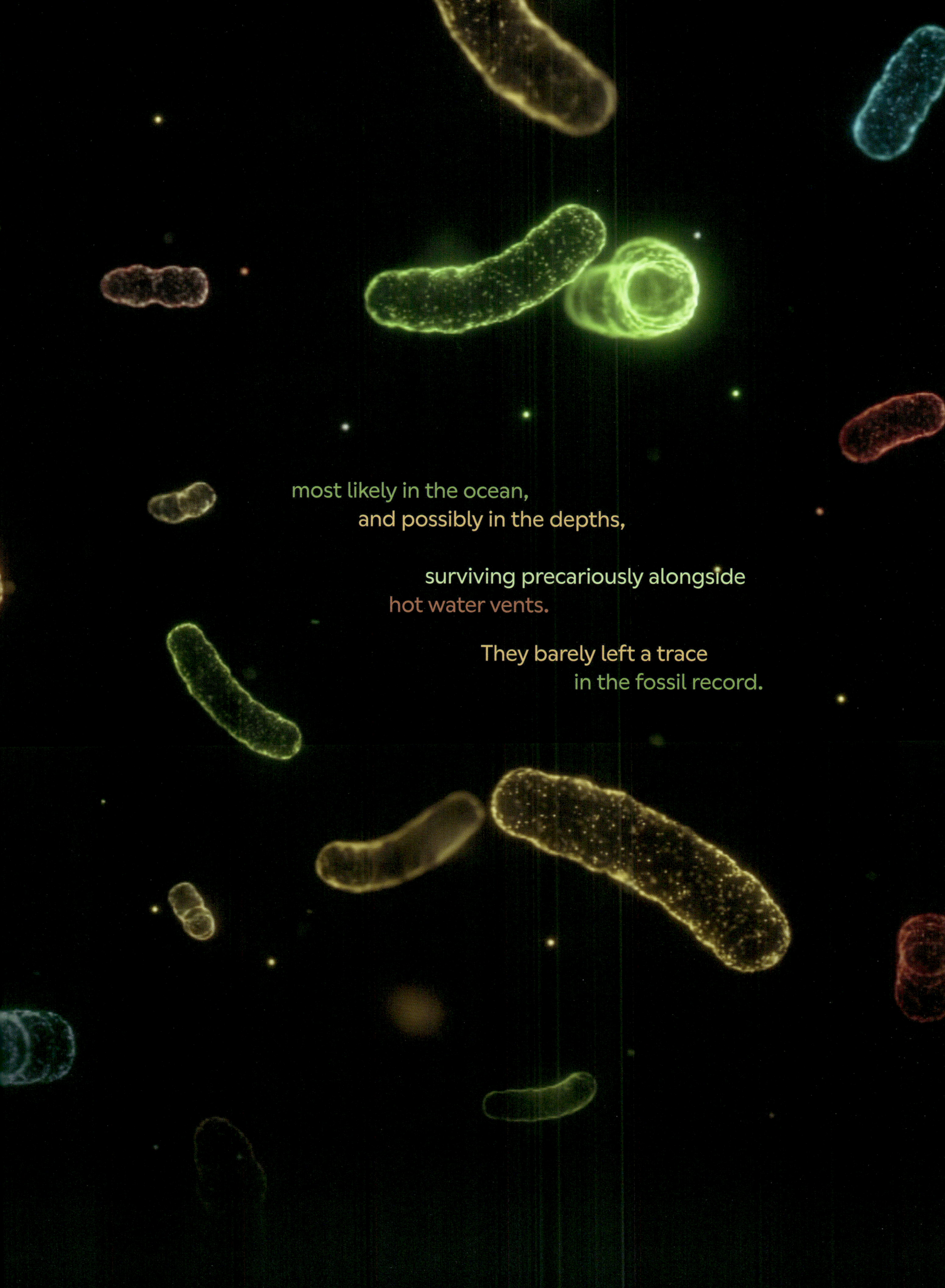

If life exists elsewhere in the universe,

this is probably

its most common form:

simple organisms surviving

in what we would consider

hostile environments.

But on Earth, life began to change, increasing in both numbers and forms, spreading over the planet.

Life has a superpower:

the ability to evolve.

This means that, over time, living things can become better and better adapted to their environment. As new life forms arose, they became ever more complex, their interactions ever more involved.

And in the process,

    Earth had become a different kind of planet.

        It was now a planet with a biosphere: a living world

that in fact made Earth

        more habitable, more stable.

But
there
were
limits
to
life's
resilience.

On at least five occasions, the Earth was swept by planetary-scale disasters. By volcanic activity strong enough to blot out the Sun and poison the seas…or an asteroid strike that sent shock waves around the globe. Millions of species disappeared at these times. Mass extinctions.

But life's superpower

meant that, each time,

the biosphere reset itself

and rebuilt...

with a **biosphere** like the one on Earth:

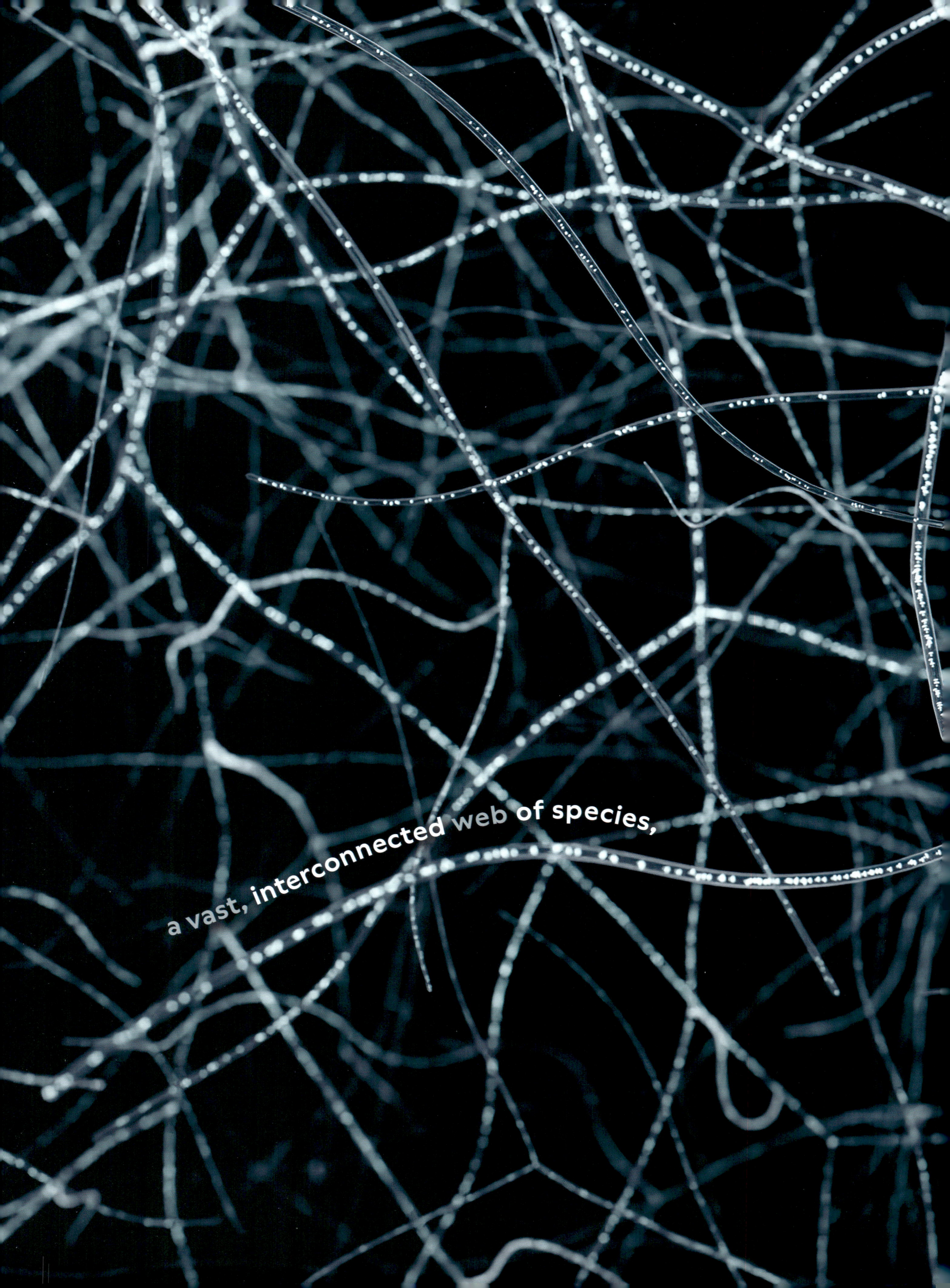

a vast, interconnected web of species,

Together,
    making use of the planet's minerals,
        creating soils rich in nutrients,

                    pooling and sharing its water,
                        creating nutrient cycles
                    that involve thousands of different organisms,

harnessing the energy
arriving from
beyond the Earth.

Earth's biosphere thrums with life: ever-changing in its composition, yet stable as a whole. We suspect that planets with biospheres as complex as this are extremely rare in the universe.

But rarer still,
is what Earth became
in its next chapter.

After the last mass extinction, sixty-six million years ago, the biosphere once again started to rebuild.

But this time, a few particularly remarkable species appeared...

Earth became home to creatures with sharp minds, strong social bonds and complex ways of communicating – much like the great apes, elephants and dolphins we know today.

Earth was now even more special in the universe – the only planet we know of with *intelligent* life.

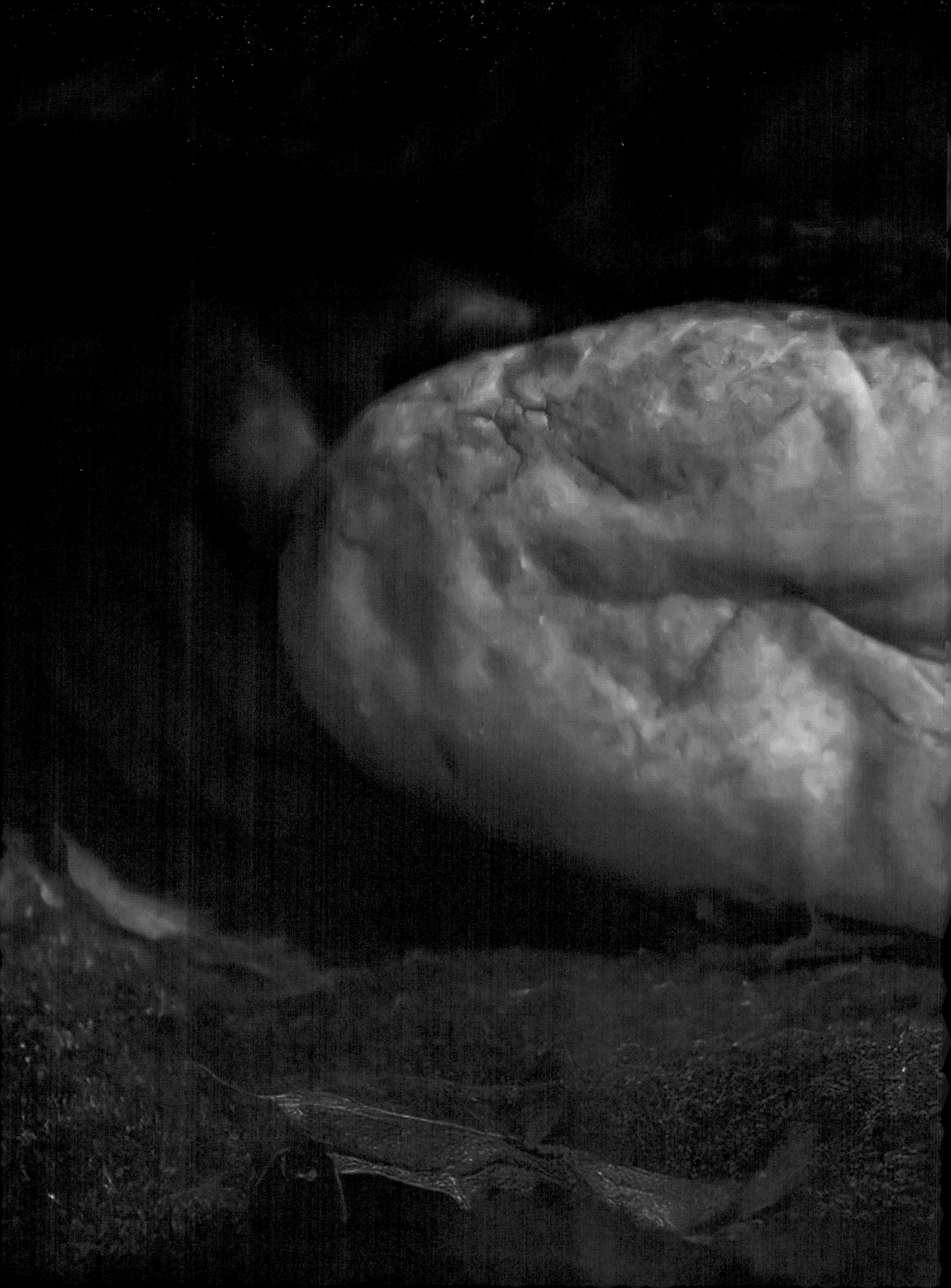

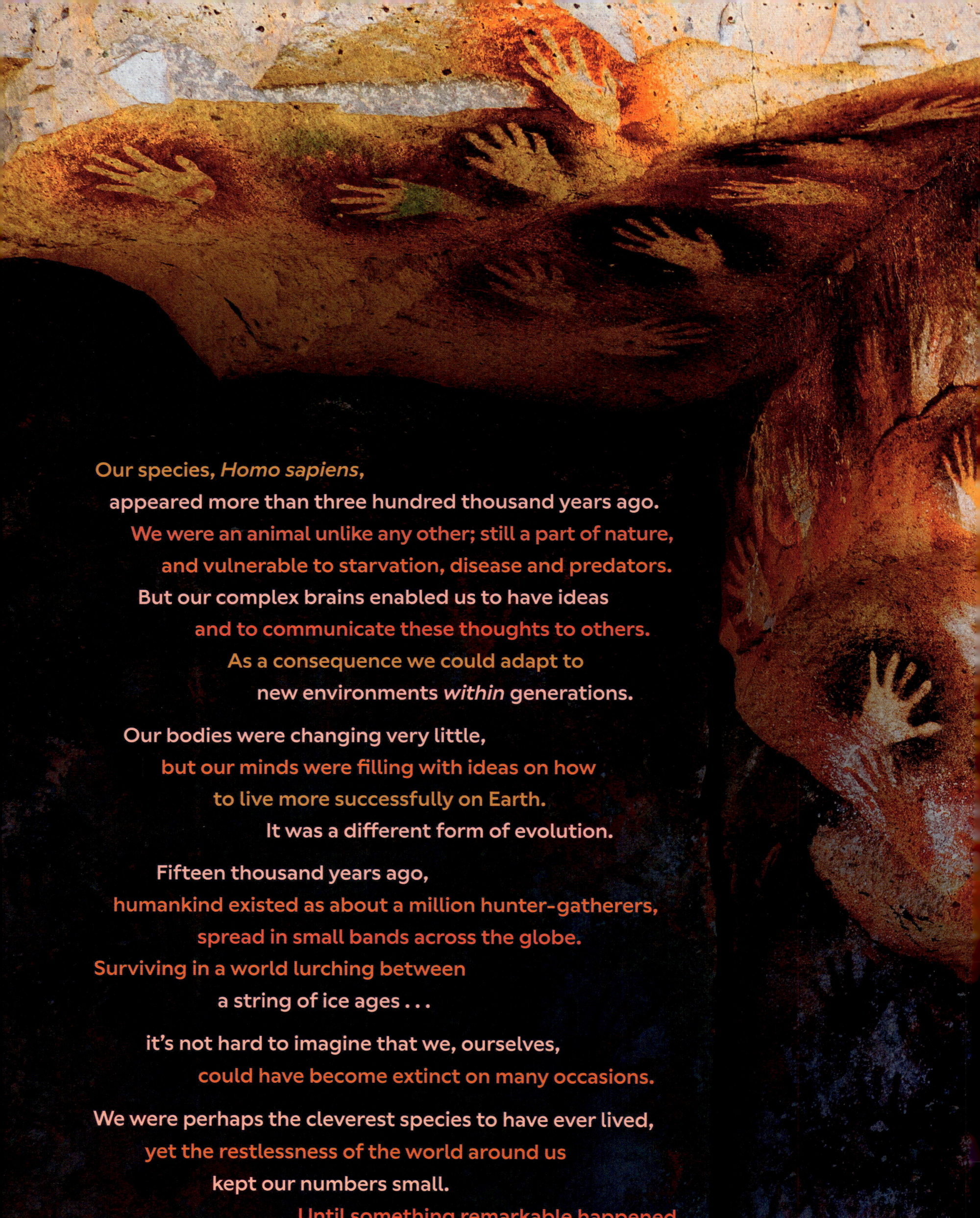

Our species, *Homo sapiens*,
  appeared more than three hundred thousand years ago.
    We were an animal unlike any other; still a part of nature,
      and vulnerable to starvation, disease and predators.
        But our complex brains enabled us to have ideas
          and to communicate these thoughts to others.
            As a consequence we could adapt to
              new environments *within* generations.

  Our bodies were changing very little,
    but our minds were filling with ideas on how
      to live more successfully on Earth.
        It was a different form of evolution.

      Fifteen thousand years ago,
        humankind existed as about a million hunter-gatherers,
          spread in small bands across the globe.
  Surviving in a world lurching between
    a string of ice ages . . .

      it's not hard to imagine that we, ourselves,
        could have become extinct on many occasions.

  We were perhaps the cleverest species to have ever lived,
    yet the restlessness of the world around us
      kept our numbers small.
        Until something remarkable happened.

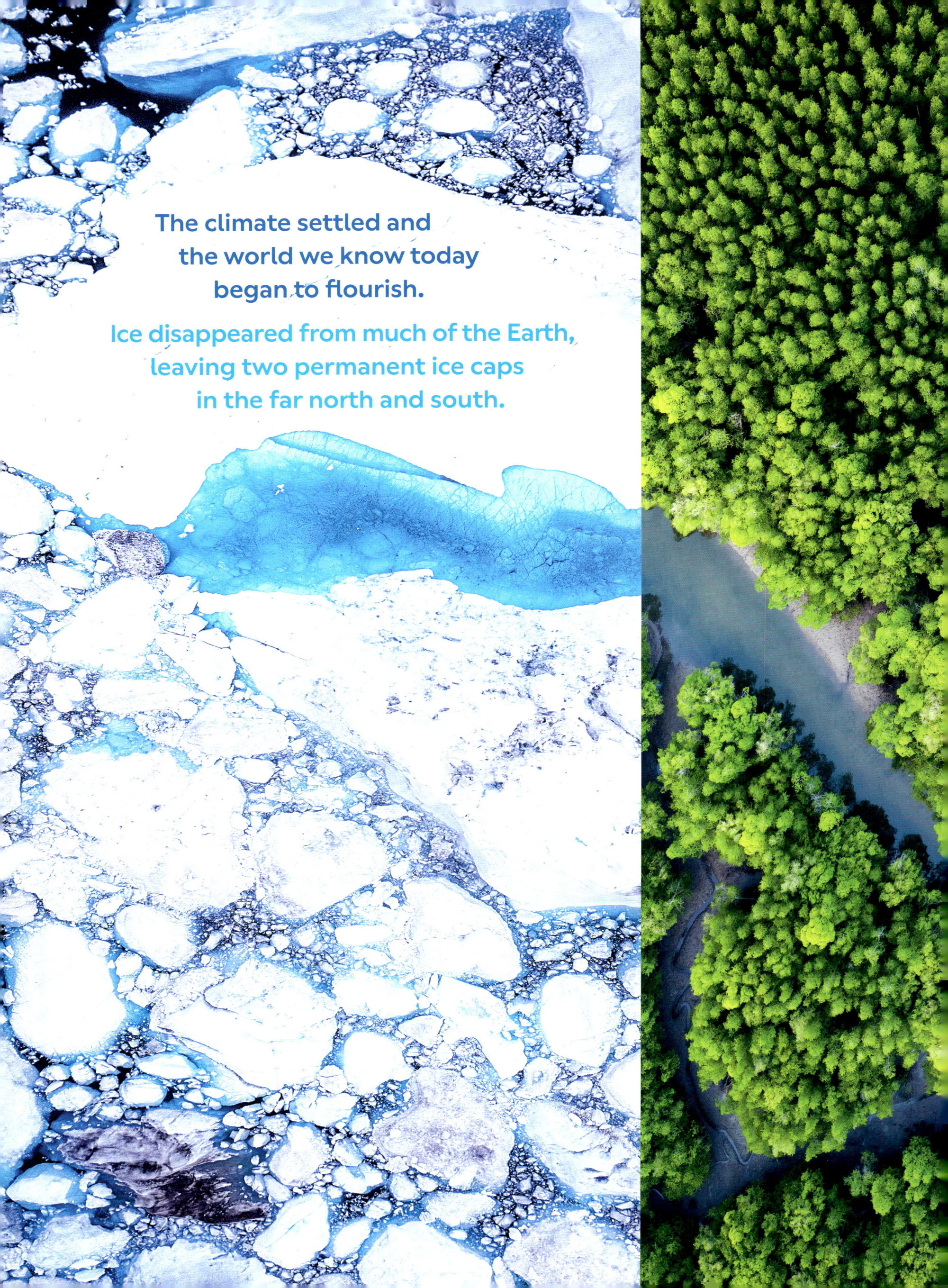

The climate settled and the world we know today began to flourish.

Ice disappeared from much of the Earth, leaving two permanent ice caps in the far north and south.

Tropical forests spanned the equator, the global ocean currents developed, coastal waters teemed with life.

Regular rains allowed the great grasslands to flourish.

Repeated conditions in spring and autumn enabled temperate forests to expand through the higher latitudes.

For over ten thousand years, the planet's average temperature did not waver more than plus or minus one degree Celsius.

Rarely in its entire history
had the Earth been so benign,
so calm,
so balanced.

All this stability allowed life to thrive,

and perhaps none did so more

than us.

In several places across the globe, groups of people took advantage of the reliable climate and settled for years on end.

They started to cultivate plants and tame animals. *Homo sapiens* had begun to learn

how to farm.

Civilisations bloomed, cities arose, human culture –
the world of our ideas – exploded!
By the earliest point in our collective living memory,
around 1920, there were almost two billion people on Earth.
We were connected as never before.
New technologies enabled us to travel and explore the globe,
and to share the experience.

It was an exciting time.

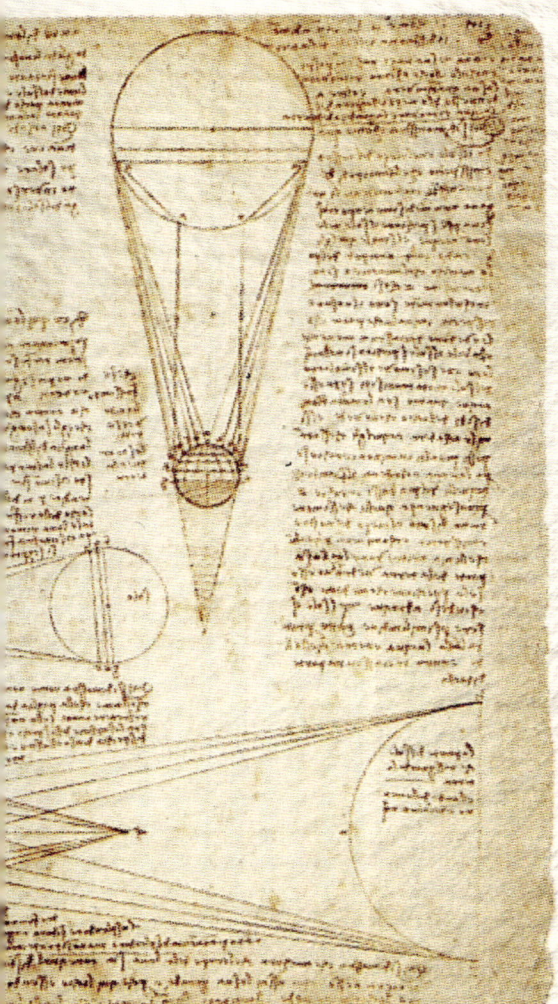

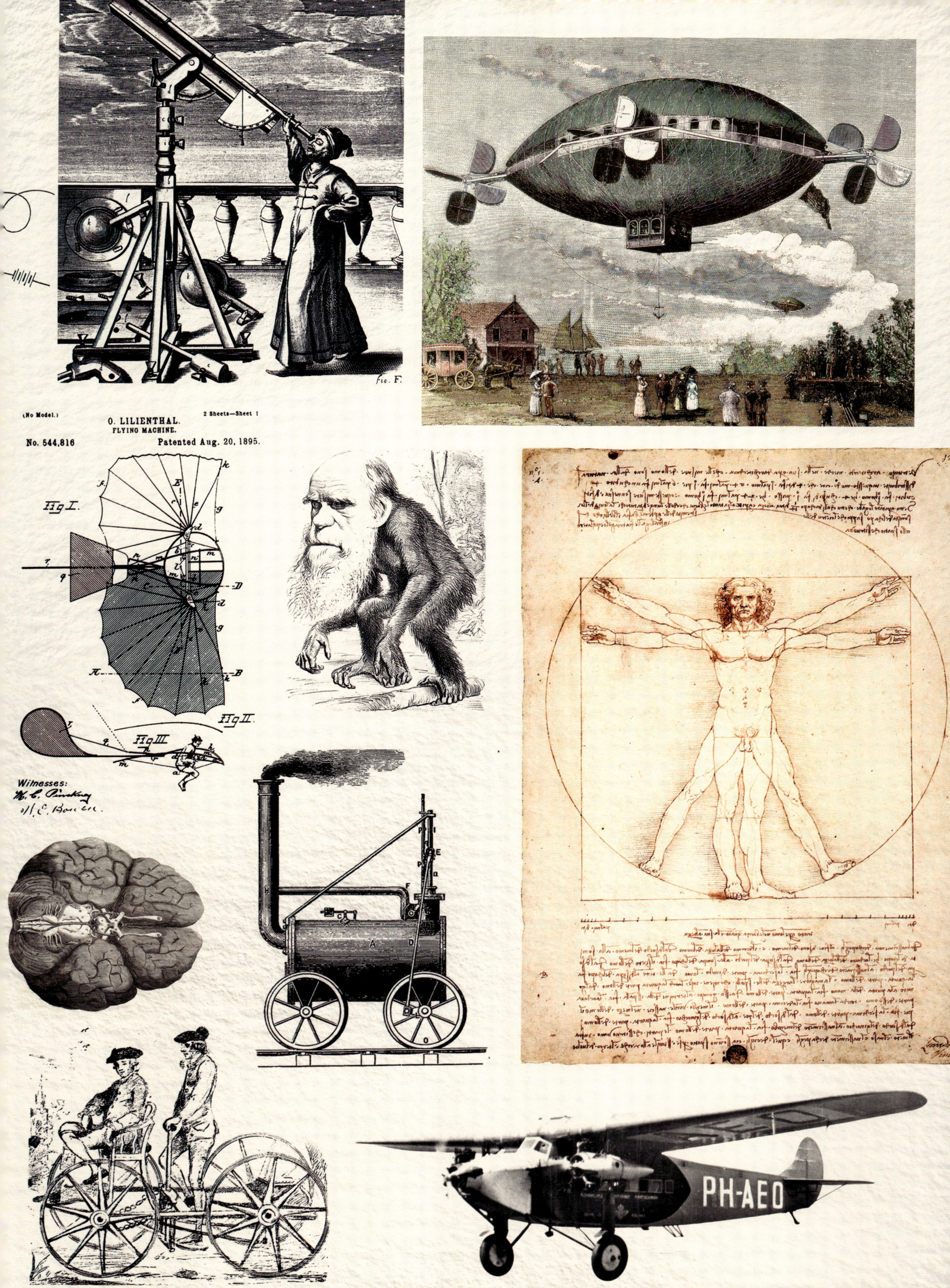

We were seeing and understanding more about our world with each passing year.

Our curiosity and ingenuity were boundless.

But amid this period of exploration and innovation came a moment that changed the tone.

In 1968, three humans left Earth's orbit for the first time.

Cameras allowed those back on Earth to share in the adventure.

Anders: Oh my God, look at that picture over there! There's the Earth comin' up. Wow, is that pretty!

Borman: Hey don't take that, it's not scheduled.

[shutter click]

Anders: You got a colour film, Jim? Hand me a roll of colour, quick, would you?

Lovell: Oh man, that's great.

Anders: Hurry.

Lovell: Where is it?

Anders: Quick.

Lovell: Down here?

Anders: Just grab me a colour. A colour exterior. Hurry up. Got one?

Lovell: Yeah, I'm lookin' for one. C 368.

Anders: Anything. Quick.

Lovell: Here.

Anders: Well, I think we missed it.

Lovell: Hey, I got it right here *[in the hatch window]*.

Anders: Let me get it out this one, it's a lot clearer.

Lovell: Bill, I got it framed, it's very clear right here!

[shutter click]

Lovell: Got it?

Anders: Yep.

Lovell: Take several, take several of 'em! Here, give it to me!

Anders: Wait a minute, just let me get the right setting here now, just calm down.

Lovell: Take—

Anders: Calm down, Lovell!

Lovell: Well, I got it right – aw, that's a beautiful shot . . . Two-fifty at f/11.

[shutter click]

We had set out to explore the Moon but what we discovered was the Earth.
With that photograph, we saw the whole of our planet for the first time,

alive, but fragile and finite.

The only place we could call home.

We began to realise that our story and our planet's story may not be aligned.
We were no longer just a clever animal finding smart ways to survive . . .

We were world-changers.

A species with the power and skill to affect the entire planet.

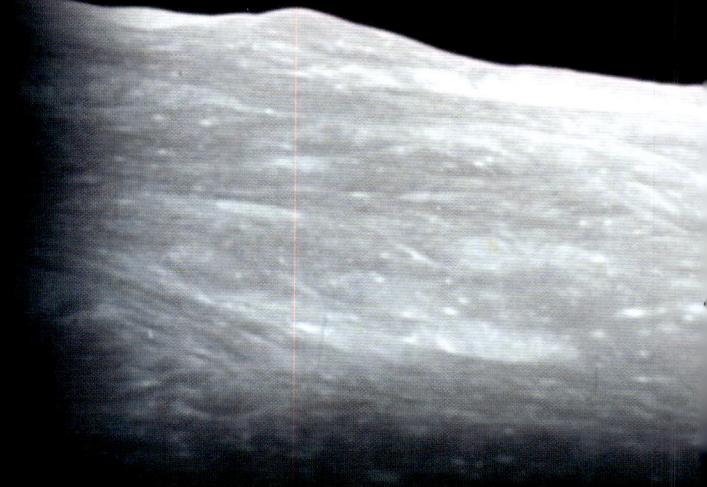

We have destroyed a third of all the forests on Earth.

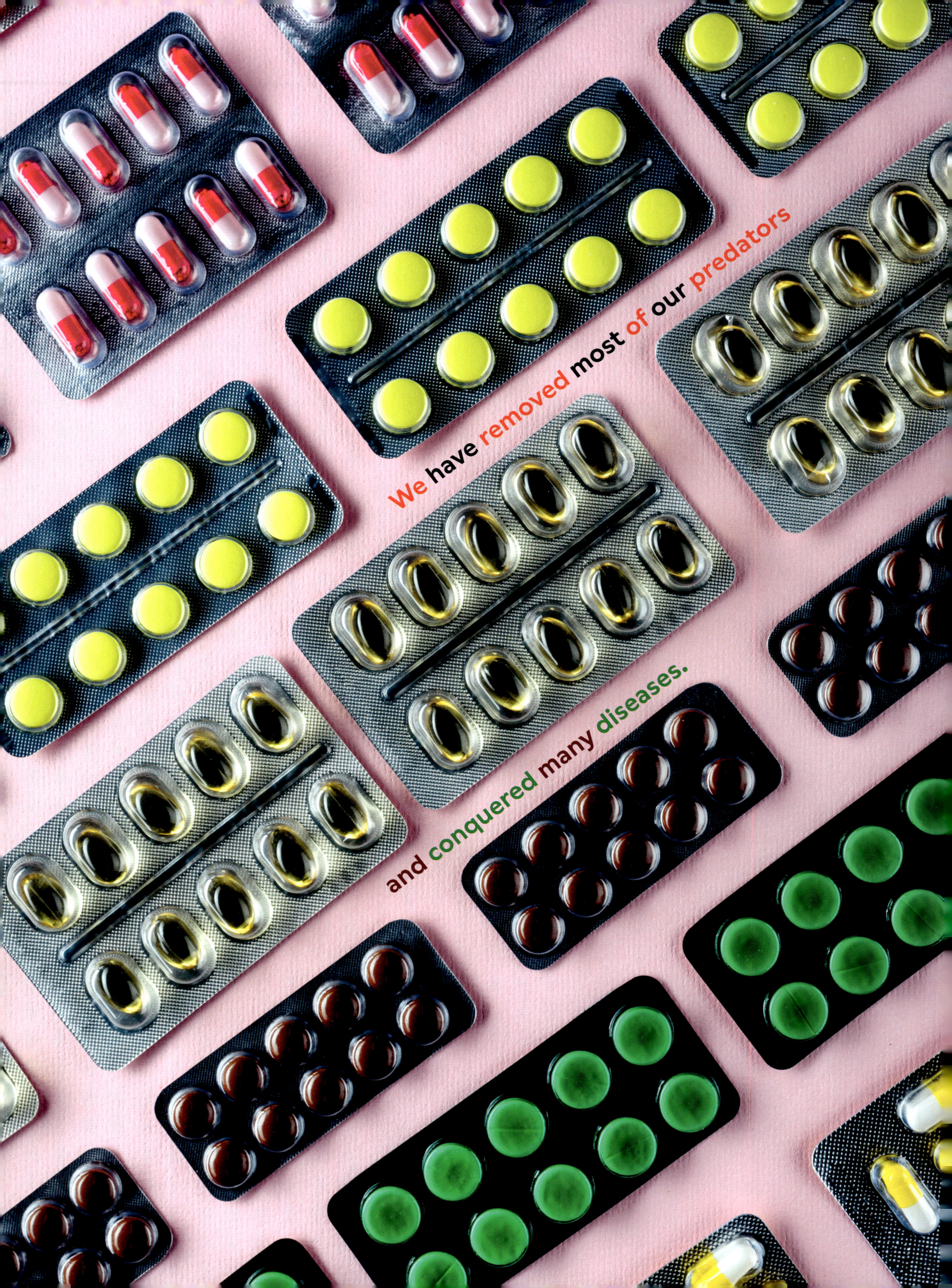

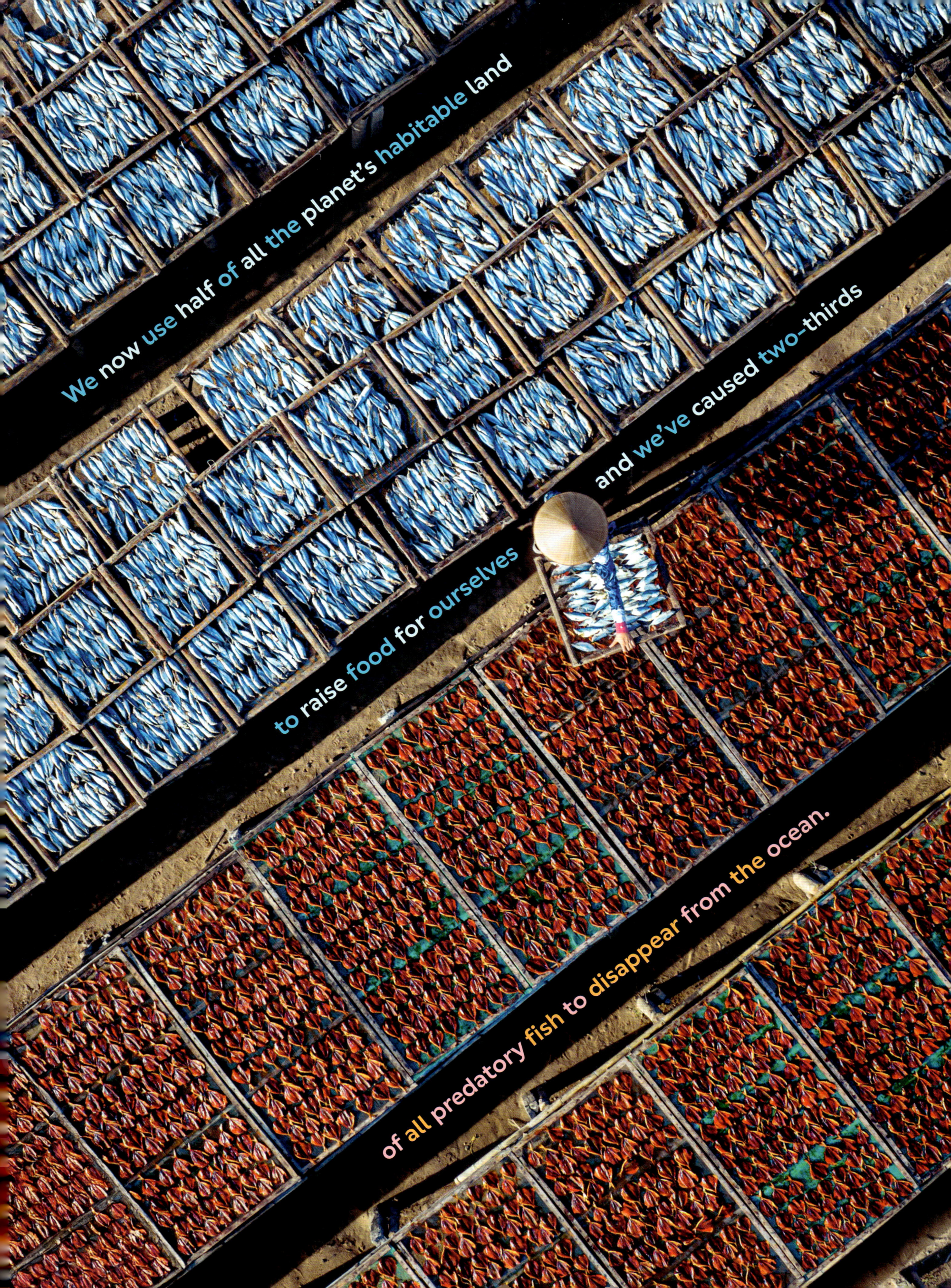

We are living creatures that have started to damage the biosphere we rely upon.

What happens next in our story?

If nothing changes, science predicts that it won't end well! We are now, in effect, acting like ancient, wayward asteroids. We are upsetting the Earth's entire system. And, just as before, the biosphere will reset – a mass extinction.

Nature will find a way to build again – it always has done. But for thousands of years, while it does so, the prospect for the generations that follow us is grim. They will be trapped on a planet that can no longer adequately support our kind.

But . . . does it have to be that way?

In the 1970s, many believed
that we were witnessing the
inevitable demise of the great whales.
After centuries of hunting, their numbers were so low,
it seemed likely they might never recover.

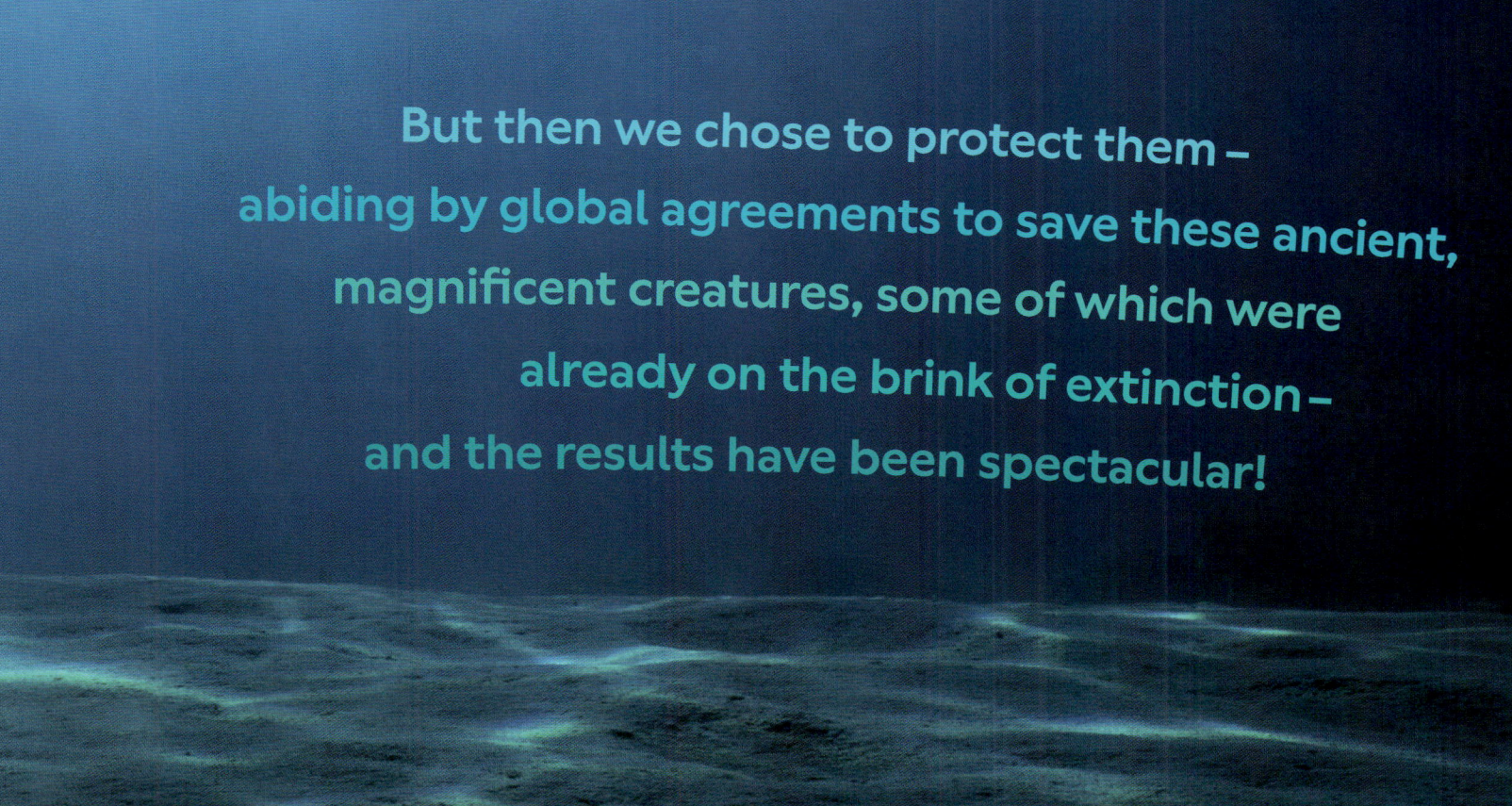

But then we chose to protect them –
abiding by global agreements to save these ancient,
magnificent creatures, some of which were
already on the brink of extinction –
and the results have been spectacular!

As some great whale populations, like the humpbacks, began to increase, we realised how important they are to life in our ocean. Whales circulate nutrients that help to create entire food chains, enabling countless other marine creatures to flourish.

The more the whales recover, the richer life in our ocean becomes, and the more we benefit. The return of the whales revealed a fundamental truth: nature is not simply beautiful, fascinating, nice to have... it is the key to our survival.

The recovery of the great whales can give us hope.

It's tempting to focus on the faults of humankind, to blame ourselves, to regard ourselves as parasites upon this beautiful planet.

But that is not the only way to see our story. Our story could also be a celebration of our gifts and our achievements, and in this telling of the story you can see us as the ultimate problem-solvers, smart enough to achieve anything we put our dazzling minds to.

That, indeed, is our superpower. So, let us use it for good.

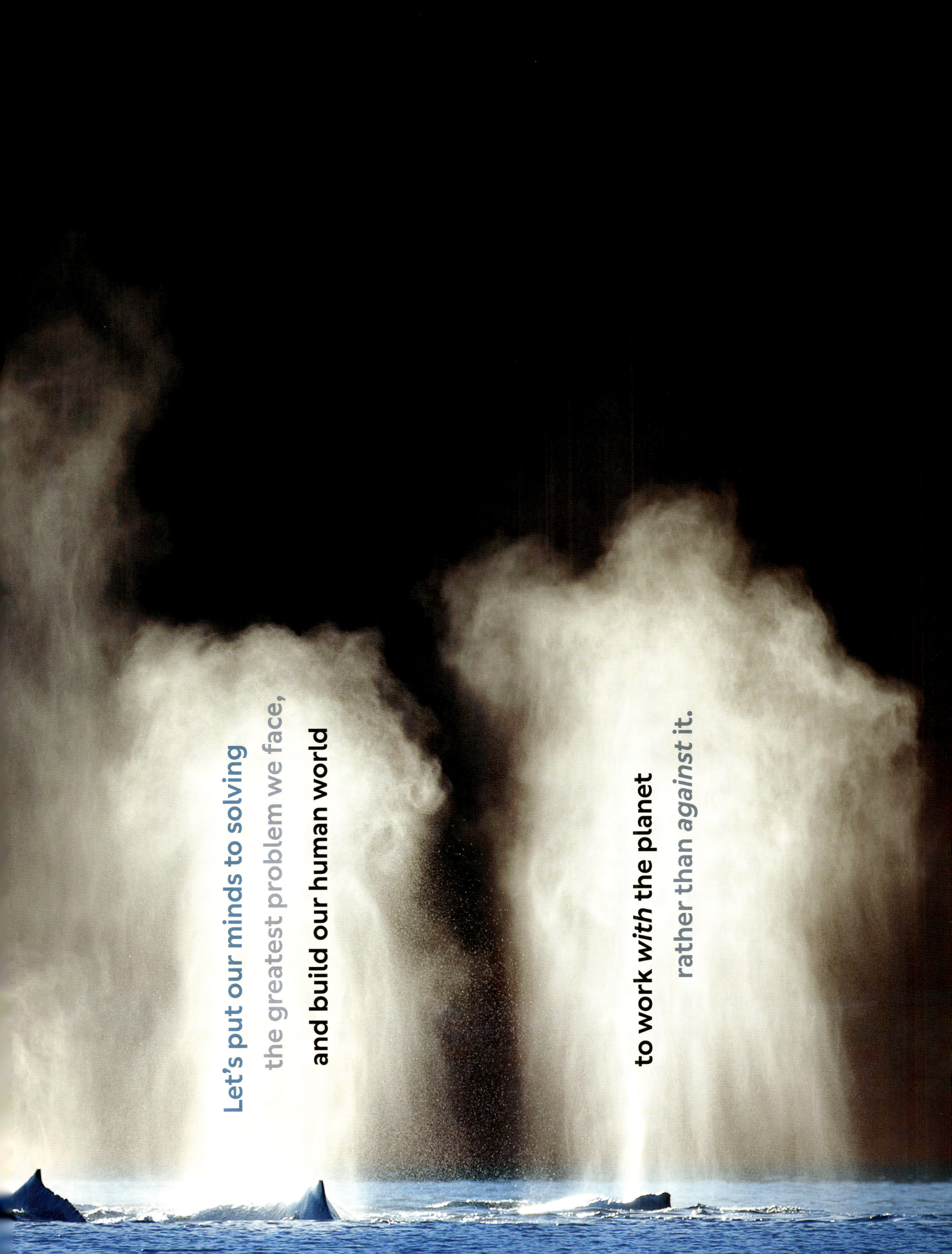

Let's put our minds to solving the greatest problem we face, and build our human world to work *with* the planet rather than *against* it.

The good news is that this work is already well under way. People around the world are coming up with the solutions we need.

A sustainable future *is* within reach.

Indeed, we can already imagine what this future would look like...

It would be a greener world.

It would be a world powered by renewable sources of energy.

The air we breathe would be cleaner.

The streets would be quieter.

Our economies and the products we use would be designed to have as little impact on nature and the climate as possible.

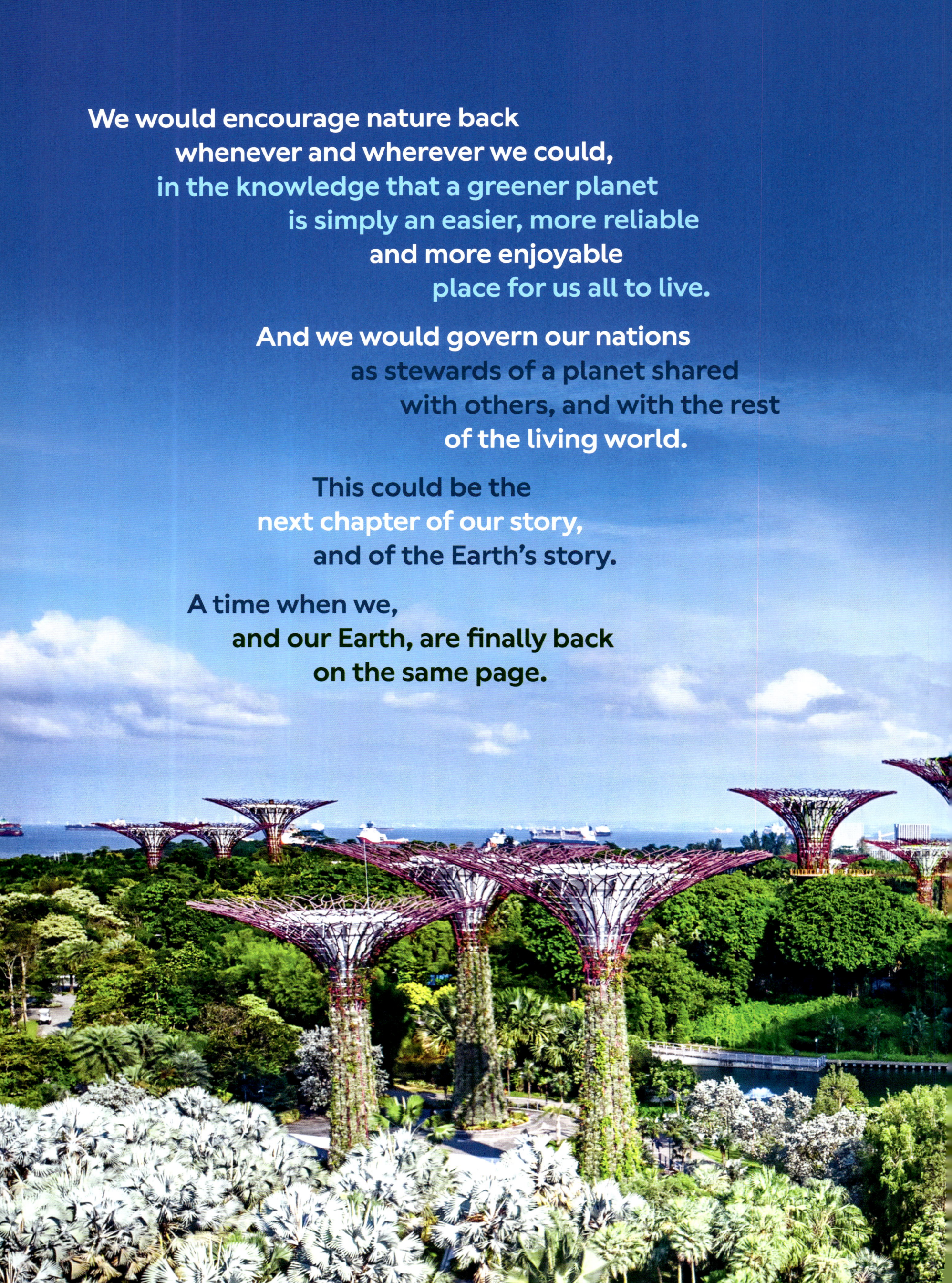

We would encourage nature back
whenever and wherever we could,
in the knowledge that a greener planet
is simply an easier, more reliable
and more enjoyable
place for us all to live.

And we would govern our nations
as stewards of a planet shared
with others, and with the rest
of the living world.

This could be the
next chapter of our story,
and of the Earth's story.

A time when we,
and our Earth, are finally back
on the same page.

When Earth becomes
that rarest thing of all:
a planet with not only an *intelligent* species,
but a *wise* one too.

Will we ever get to this place?
Only *you* can answer that question.

Of the one hundred billion or so humans
that have ever existed,
it's only those alive today
that can build this future.

It is a huge challenge,
but if we cooperate
and communicate –
as only humans can –
we have the most wonderful world
to look forward to.

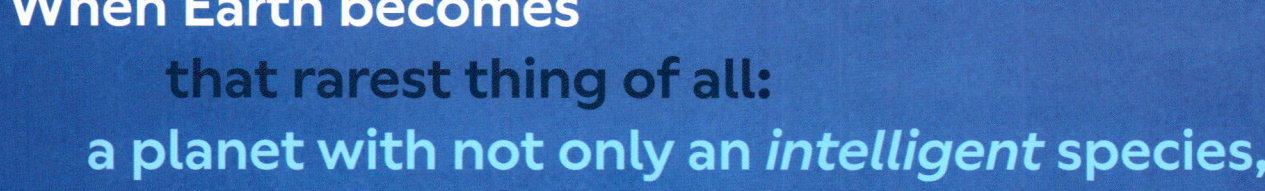

You have the opportunity to help write
    the next chapter in our story,

and you have the whole
    of our natural world,

billions of years in the making,

as your ally.

NOW is the most exciting time
        in history to be alive.

For in the vastness of space,
    the unimaginable extents of time,

YOUR LIFE IS TRULY SIGNIFICANT